Ian Ralphs
Poems for a Hanging

Poems and photographs by Ian Ralphs

Drawings by Becky Martin

REAL WORLD
Abram's Bridge, Stoke-on-Trent

First published in Great Britain by Real World 1997

All poems copyright Ian Ralphs 1997

All drawings by Becky Martin

All photographs by Ian Ralphs

Mono relief print for "Infrared Highwayman"
by Hilary Jefferies

Typeset and layout by Ian Ralphs

Ian Ralphs asserts the moral right to
be identified as the author of this work

The copyright on all illustrations is owned
by Ian Ralphs

Front cover etched relief print by Hilary Jefferies
from an original photograph by Ian Ralphs

Back cover photograph by Ian Ralphs

Printed in Great Britain by
Stowes *the* Printers
Park Hall Works
Sutherland Road
Longton
Stoke- On- Trent

A CIP record for this book is
available from the British Library

ISBN 0 9530797 0 8

All rights reserved. No part of this publication may be
reproduced, stored in a retrieval system, or transmitted
in any form or by any means, electrical, mechanical,
photocopying, recording or otherwise, without the prior
permission of the copyright holder.

To Rachel

with undying love

This is reality

Today, men proclaimed the world
ends tomorrow, despite the fact
it ended today

DAVID EDWARDS

"Without You"

THURSDAY 7 AM	2.
LAST EXCURSION	3.
WHITEBRIDGE LANE	4.
GIRL WITH STRAWBERRY EYES	6.
SISTER	8.
BROTHER BEYOND	9.
TRAINSPOTTING	10.
PRAYER FOR MATHILDA	11.
UNDERCLASS	12.
CHEADLE DREAM CATCHER	14.
NORTON BRIDGE	15.
PLASTIC SMILE?	16.
WENGERNALP	17.
LAST EIGHT	18.
THE SIDE-STAND	18.
SUMMER 1991	20.
RIVER	22.
NIGHT SWEEPER	23.
SONG FOR RICHEY MANIC	24.
POSTCARD FROM THE EDGE OF TOWN	25.
THURSDAY 7 PM	26.
MANDARIN TIN	27.
GOIN' NOWHERE	28.
DOWN BY THE CHURCH STREET GARDENS	30.
MISS ADVENTURE	32.
NOCTURNE	33.
CANDLE SONG	36.
REALITIES	37.
PEARL WHITE EIGHT	38.
SUMMER 1995	39.
AUGUST 16th 1993	40.
RUNAWAY GIRL	42.
BLACK ROSES	43.
NURSE	44.
HAIKU TIME	45.
LAST DREAM	46.
INFRARED HIGHWAYMAN	48.

THURSDAY 7 AM

My clock has stopped.
I always forget to wind it up.
I only bought it because it's like yours.
And so I'm washed up on Neigwl,
Still wearing the shirt I stole from your room,
The smell of you still on it.
Sometimes I dream I'm your lover,
Sobbing fears onto your warm shoulder,
Kissing your slim white stomach,
Wishing to be in there, unborn.
At night, my tie- dyes become
A womb of jellied colours,
Pulling me into foetal dreams;
My books go back to being trees,
Their branches scratching at the walls,
Knocking ornaments off shelves,
Breaking glass.
One morning,
As I thread through
The dusty yellows
Of desire,
I will wake,
To the ticking of your clock,
And you.

LAST EXCURSION

I remember the evening sun
Through the freckles of dirt on the carriage window
As we left London behind;
The flashing past of station names
I knew only from travel guides;
The silver song of the rails
Cooling slowly in the humid evening.
Hot coffee, strawberries,
Grandad pointing out the lights of Birmingham
As passengers mingled in the corridors.
I recall having energy to spare
On the walk from Stone station
As I ran through the green lights and trees
Of Newcastle Road,
Four hours after my bed time.
I think back to deep sleep among
Dreams of permanence
Where the same silver songs
Took me away
To foreign lands I'd never seen.
I remember being loved.

WHITEBRIDGE LANE

The bridge was gone.
There were still no steps down to the canal.
The towpath was a tightrope
Where there'd once been a road.
Willows still dipped their hair in the water,
But too many years
Had washed away all trace of beauty.
And through the long grass,
I acted out one of our old football games,
Kicking a rusty can into the rubble
That used to be a factory.
Goal! ...
I skimmed stones at absent boats,
Serenading absent friends
With tuneless whistles
As the sun perished
Behind John Simon's house,
Crashing dull orange
Through the orchards beyond;
No splendour followed
As I stumbled through
The smoke of
Forgotten firework shows;
The bonfire still
Burning away the gold
Outside the crowded house.
I should have known better
Than to walk
Where once I had disappeared...
They found my car by the bridge.

GIRL WITH STRAWBERRY EYES

She's an image on my wall,
Framed by carved wooden edelweiss.
She's my lamented idol:
My Ingrid Bergman with
Polly Harvey hair,
Seventeen and radiant.
She's *Tramp* perfume,
Opium candles and autumn skies,
A faded Tintinara dress,
Mascara kisses
And strawberry eyes.
For a moment
I beheld her,
As she moved through the fair
On 16mm Kodachrome,
Smelt the fresh
Colours in her hair,
As she lay with me,
A punk on the run from home.
Three years hence,
Her tears
Still soak my pillow.

SISTER

When I look at you,
My fragile world is all yours;
Your smile,
Is the sun in my sky,
The reason why,
I believe in love again today.
Sister,
When you're away,
You become sister moon,
Illuminating my tiny room;
When I cry,
Your voice sings a soft lullaby;
The shepherdess of my sleep,
You close my eyes
And count my sheep;
In my worried dream
You chase away all evil
Before I scream;
You clasp me tight,
Protect me from the fight,
Guide me in the dark
And save me from the shark;
And when I need to rest my head,
I dream of lying in the red
Silk-screen roses of your bed.
You're my blanket on a winter's night,
My eternal angel wrapped in white,
My one and only antidote
To the worlds' harms,
Forever there to catch me,
As I fall again,
Naked,
Alone and helpless
Into your arms.

BROTHER BEYOND

To an overture of clanging and endless beat upon beat upon beat of the great machine, from his basket of fresh five pound notes high above the factory sub- troposphere, where layer upon layer

upon layer of artificial clouds stretch out like bloody entrails set in precipitous amber; where the skylights have turned to tachylite black and acetylene lights flicker like cine movies of incendiary fires in the

blitz, my brother stands and dreams of the horses at Fakenham.

TRAINSPOTTING

A graveyard of frosted windows.
Yellow paint oxidising.
Royal blue livery turned
White in neglect.
No track ahead, no train behind,
Behold,
The terminated line.
Acres of wasting steel
And fraying asbestos
With nowhere to go,
No passengers to haul,
No buffers to cushion
The blow:
A funeral line of man's
Discarded invention;
Forty exhausts that blew
Whistling diesel fumes:
Clouds of black,
Pounding the great roof
Above Crewe station,
Now echoing only
To the chatter of crows,
Nests protruding like fungi
On a hollow tree.
The blow- torch awaits
Like the angel of death,
Beckoning
To old ladies in rest homes;
Ivernia, Mauritania, Apapa,
Names as obsolete
As the forsaken wrecks in this
Temple of metallic bones;
As an electric arcs far below me,
On the fast main line,
I turn from Eagle Bridge,
My head full of sadness,
My notebook empty this time.

PRAYER FOR MATHILDA
(Inspired by the movie "Leon")

Mathilda please don't cry alone,
My little girl lost without a home,
Call me your brother, call me your dad,
Call me anytime to shelter you,
From this dreadful life you've had.

OK

Mathilda let me take away your pain,
Teach you to laugh and smile again,
With each tear that falls on my shirt:
One tear less to shed, a second less to hurt;
Let me be your hero, let me be your clown,
I'll be here to love and hold you,
Whenever you're feeling down.

OK

Mathilda let me fill your life with light,
Darksome angel become angel bright,
Let my humble house become your home,
No more walking late into the night,
Our two hearts together alone.

OK

Mathilda I promise to be true,
I know how your family treated you,
No more arguments, no more fears,
I truly love you for all your tender years;
Call me your brother, call me your dad,
Sweet child alone,
I'll call you my very own,
Destiny,
The daughter I never had.

OK

UNDERCLASS

He's the king of the scrap yard heap,
Owns no silver or crystal glass,
His family were the leisure society,
But he skipped school too often,
With the boys from the underclass.

Tonight he's soaked in dirt,
Stuffing coiled copper wire
Up his filthy shirt,
Stealing poor mans' riches,
On pitch- black nights,
In a world of guard dogs,
Alarm bells and blue lights.

He's the king of the non- statistical,
Stealing the dead man's car
After the crash;
His family were the lazy bourgeoisie,
But 'round here,
He's the unwritten law:
A parasite
Of the underclass.

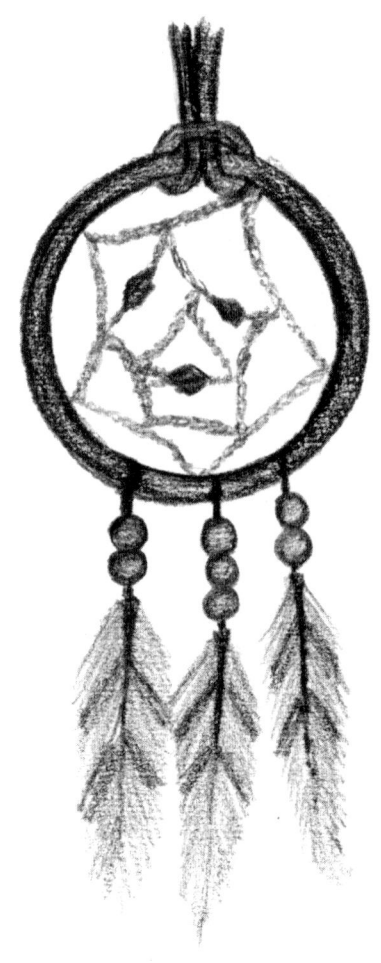

CHEADLE DREAM CATCHER

Low- down hillside kingfisher stream,
Take my soul and catch my dream;
Blueberry borage Church Street tree,
Catch my spirit and set me free;
To run with those I love but see no more,
To send black flowers to a far distant shore.
So let the church bells take my scream,
Low- down hillside kingfisher stream,
Lost dreams, Rachel and me,
Here forever 'neath this willow tree.

NORTON BRIDGE

1991

Pollen breeze follow me,
Where the grasshopper lies,
And lapwings and
B- 52s
Trace the skies.

1993

Spring light,
Before the blur,
My motorcycle at evening,
And her.

1994

Time to reflect,
To regret;
To idle in
Wilderness.

1995

Infinite memories,
Tunnel freight,
A curlew calling,
Too late, too late.

1996

An empty heart,
Metal sea,
Ghosts in ice,
Endlessly.

PLASTIC SMILE?

I saw that effigy, the skeleton you carved from
credit cards: the one that gave you all those
adjectives and accents. I saw it placed on your

polished shelf next to a Polaroid of your smiling
father. How long did it last? Time enough to show
off your new found wealth in the park on a high,

until you returned one evening and remembered
the derelict terraces of Priory Road and sent it back
in an envelope marked fragile. *Good on you*

I said. But did I really mean it? No more tequila.
No more cigar ash in the Nelson ashtray. No more
plunging neck lines and rolled gold. *It doesn't buy*

happiness your dad wrote in his finest hand on
Basildon paper. You cried.

Explain that to me will you please.

WENGERNALP

Expresso at altitude.
Menthol *North Poles* in cold foil.
Burning sun.
The whir of the slow, empty train,
Winding away
To the huskies
And the hollow shadows of Eigergletscher.
Alone at last.
This white- out psychedelia is mine:
Gold silhouettes of
Cities in icing sugar and
Clementines
Fossilised in rock face;
Black ravines
Of splintered glass
Separate me,
Freeze and
Phase me
In silent awe;
The heroes of
The Lauberhorn are gone,
The ski- lifts
Wasting
In summer sun,
As I forage amber slopes
Of salad grass
In search of orchids;
Not a cloud,
Nor a soul,
Or a question
To ask -
Only my own impermanence.
The apples here
Taste the same as
Those in Grandad's orchard,
A thousand miles away.

LAST EIGHT

It was an eight.
I found it in the corner of the room
Covered in dust.
At least I thought it was an eight.
I wiped it with a soft cloth,
But it was stained with something.
I left it there a few days,
Picked it up sometimes,
Looked at it.
One day I took it to my friend,
She said,
It's just an eight, Ian,
What's so special about an eight?
Then I remembered...
Took it home,
Hid it away.

THE SIDE-STAND

I swore.
Said it was so cheap
It must be made of chocolate;
Perhaps only tin foil chrome
Wrapped around the stems
Of spring flowers;
You laughed.
Said it was fine.
I slept.

SUMMER 1991

Pouring rain magnified the crimsons and the azure,
Gave way to firefly sunshine and a river running dry,
Looking back from years ago I smiled,
And the laughter echoed on into the night,
Long after the thunder had gone.
The morning glory proclaimed new angels above,
And I rested a while,
Oblivious as I was to the stories yet to be told,
I worked on into the twilight.
I, the late night gardener in splintered prisms of ultraviolet:
The stars and stripes of a David Wheaton bandanna,
A faded Louisiana baseball shirt and Agassi shorts;
Disguises I would one day rescue from my drawer,
As my eyes burned in the glow of nostalgia;
I, the poet, unable to find again my hallowed lawn,
The lone colour plate in the book of my life,
That rests on a shelf no- one can reach.

RIVER

River,
Take me back along the paths of my past,
All those lonely summers,
I knew they would never last.

River,
Be the soft rhythm behind my song,
Sail me away from this land
Where I belong.

River,
Erode away my blackened heart,
Wash away the bitterness
That fills my soul
And tears me apart.

River,
Meander quietly
Through these fields of wild flowers;
The meadow,
The lilies,
The night jar:
This unsung paradise,
Is ours.

NIGHT SWEEPER

Can you hear his soft invasion?
Acoustic leaves scratching in the dusk of the Midway,
Yellows and crimsons and voices under trees,
Perished marigolds, archways, reveries.

Can you see his dark shadow?
An actor devoid of light, with a barrow full of stars,
Collecting the death masks of summer:
A blood rose, an old gramophone, a frozen vase.

Did you see the night sweeper
Dancing in the dying November sun;
Hitting two- handed backhand drives
Into silent beds where no flower survives?
Did you marvel at his art,
Or wonder if it hides a broken heart?
Did you stop for a moment to consider his plight,
As he swept away the garments
Of a whole splendid summer
In one night?

SONG FOR RICHEY MANIC

Saw a young girl crying
On the hillside where I walk at night
Stopped and sat with her a while
A kind of dark angel with no smile
Distortion in white

Saw blood soaked in her dress
Initials and hearts carved by her own hand
Black flowers of pain and distress
The world's greatest rock band

She grabbed me and looked into my eyes
She yelled Richey lives Richey gives
Then Richey dies
And I told her she must be strong enough to burn
'Cause sometimes even the disappeared return

Together we threw black petals in the stream
And dried each others' tears
We said we'd listen for his music in dreams
For the rest of our years

And I carried her home
Put her to bed beneath a picture of his face
Her parents told me they didn't know why
She'd ever want to die
And I spoke not of death
But of the love she'd somehow found
In such a darkened place

POSTCARD FROM THE EDGE OF TOWN

It's July,
But here on the edge of town
I can find only autumn.
In my garden,
Sycamore trees
With their dried leaves,
Whisper like high baskets
Of waste paper in the wind,
As the waterfall drowns me
In rhymes that drift
And snag my curtains,
Then perish
In radio silences of ultramarine.
After nightfall,
Freight trains from Lackenby
Thunder past my open window,
Waking ghosts in photographs,
Running on towards the city,
Pulled by the glow
Of the steel works and retail parks;
And I know you must hear them,
As they pass by your house
In the shadow of the concrete overpass;
So I lie here in my bed,
Coding messages for you
In the clatter of the trucks,
As diesel fumes float by,
Black as coffee.
Sometimes,
In the early hours,
I stand on the platform
Where I once held you
As trains go by,
Wondering still
If you should ever wonder why
I'm still here.

THURSDAY 7 PM

Some say I hurt myself,
But what would they know?
How many times have they dreamed
Of being lost and not caring where they are,
Only to wake, panic stricken in their own bed?
Have they ever dreamed of their lost love,
Running, laughing and smiling
Through the clear running streams of yesterday
That freeze and turn to ice as they wake,
Then disappear?
Are their hearts made of glass too?
And if so do they shatter like mine?
And do the fragments slide down
Into their stomach during the night,
To lie there, jagged and waiting
For dreams end?
In the movements of another day
In this real life that is over in a blink,
Do they ever stop to look,
To think,
To question?
Or perhaps to hear someone say,
He hurts himself.

MANDARIN TIN

Sellotape snagged on torn wrapping paper;
compressed, ragged.
Ribbons scrunched like wire, tangling like
discarded sheep's wool.
A tag, string, still tied.
An envelope, tiny, empty now.
A quote, meaningless to many:
Love.
Additional remnants of paper, ripped:
Excess to all but me;
Clothes discarded before my eyes,
Now safe in darkness,
Like thoughts,
They wear a thin disguise.
I only have this tinder- box
To warm my secret heart,
As waves of darkness
Sweep me out to sea,
Tearing all that's left of me
Irreparably apart.
Within my mandarin tin
Lies evidence:
Once I was safe and warm,
Desirable,
A song just begun;
A butterfly flying,
Slowly dying,
In the pale light of a winter sun.

GOIN' NOWHERE (SONG)

Well I'm ridin' through your old town
Just as I do every night
I'm On Fire cracklin' through my earphones
And I can pretend everything's all right
But there aint no flames out here baby
On this cold damp road
And I remember you disappeared
So long ago

And I'm goin' crazy baby
I don't know what else to do
So I ride this machine
Into the night
'Cause I'm still missin' you
And I'm goin' nowhere
Goin' nowhere
That's where you'll find me
Searchin' for you

I remember back in '94
Well you called me on the phone
Said you needed to see me
Said you felt all alone
So I rode out into the night
Found you sittin' there
I held you tight
And gave you a ride home

Well I wish I'd seen the future, girl
'Cause I never would have let you go
Now I ride past your house
In the middle of the night
Girl, I've never felt so alone

And I'm goin' crazy baby
I don't know what else to do
So I ride this machine
Into the night
'Cause I'm still in love with you
And you're goin' nowhere
Goin' nowhere
You're stayin' here with me
When I find you

DOWN BY THE CHURCH STREET GARDENS

Down by the Church Street Gardens I met a young girl so fair,
We walked together in the ruins when no-one lived there,
By archways shrouded in rhododendrons out of sight,
She would lead me down the supernatural corridors of the night.

Sitting by The Terrace where coaches used to stop by,
She spoke of ghosts of horsemen and spirits in the sky,
Sometimes I'd chase her behind fallen pillars in the tall grass,
And lying in her arms many happy hours would come to pass.

In a world of hanging gardens overgrown with blossom and vines,
We found our tangled paradise in the decaying grandeur of regal lines,
Speaking with her eyes she once revealed she was dead,
But she was my Giselle and I adored her sweet tormented head.

One night she turned to me and spoke of impending fear,
I hushed her and cradling her in my arms she pulled me near,
Making love in a high empty bedroom under our dreamtime sky,
She whispered, "Good-bye, my beloved, my spook, good-bye."

In the daytime a ravaging blaze swept my love away in a funeral pyre,
A lost scream in the empty galleries as the flames grew ever higher,
One day time will lift my head as I walk in anguish and shame,
Long before I cease to wander in the darkness still calling her name.

MISS ADVENTURE

She never saw the light; just blurred twinkling stars
Through windows in fast cars in the night.
Slowly, she became a vixen of icy games,
Amphetamines and false names whispered
In rooms out of sight.
She thought they loved her: enchantment by pure desire;
But the masquerade was too old
For a fable bought and sold
By a physical and spiritual liar.
In her mirror she still saw the eyes of a child:
A spell of innocence in which they'd surely drown;
But all they saw was something gone wild,
So they took her away,
And they ran her down;
They just took her,
And ran her down.

NOCTURNE

Myra Ellen chords,
Floating,
In the stillness
Of the night air;
You,
Bringing me
Flowers for the night,
And sandalwood
Beads to wear;
Chess pieces,
Scattered,
From my losing
Endgame;
Valentines,
Silvery
In the soil
Where I engraved
Your name;
You laughed,
When I stood
In the road,
Reciting
My red wine Blake,
But the song
Of your laughter
Woke me
From my sadness
And kept me awake;
And when your ghouls
Visited,
I sheltered you,
With my midnight
Overcoat;
And as I watched,
Your eyes
Turn to glass,
To you
These words
I wrote;

I kissed
Your lips,
Pushed back
Your soft,
Coloured hair,
But you never
Felt me,
Or heard my
Silent Lucidity
As you slept
In strange rhythms,
Unaware;
And as the
Unreflected
Portrait
Drifted
Across the clovers
Of the croquet lawn,
I knew
I could never
Wish for more
Than our love:
A vision
Blessed by angels,
Yet alas,
My dear Rachel,
A dream forlorn.

CANDLE SONG

Lonely candle burning white,
Be my flickering friend tonight,
My companions they all have fled,
My lilies and roses lie strewn and dead.

Lonely candle burning yellow,
Light the lines of *Macbeth* and *Othello*,
Tragedies of words that shaped my life,
Romantic intrigue and death by the knife.

Lonely candle burning blue,
Sadness takes the forsaken few,
Silent witness to my futile shout,
Sister darkness will take me,
As the flame dies out.

Lonely candle charred and black,
Now I know I can't turn back,
Expiring in the world within my room,
Like me you once stood tall,
Like you I burned out too soon.

REALITIES

I

Where no- one finds me in my tie- dyes,
As dewberries send me to sleep with open eyes;
Black nightshade engulfs me,
She runs laughing and says she won't ever love me;
My eyes blur but she stays out in the rain,
Until my telephone rings and I fight consciousness,
And she hangs up again.

II

Where my clock still shows seven minutes past four,
And my college books sit unread;
Where the lights of Cheadle Road beckon me
Out into the night beyond the moonchimes,
To roar down into the valley,
Where the noise of my engine
Cuts the night air like a great scythe
But no- one listens.
Where I'm a ghost rider in an old movie
Thrown and lost in her wishing well,
Along with my old shirts, tapes and postcards.

III

Where I become her,
Searching for me,
Tired and lonely,
By cold running streams:
Lost dreams,
Ours only.

PEARL WHITE EIGHT

Sometimes she's a distant pylon on a hill; wires leading to another, then another, wound up on bobbins in some electric silk mill. She's the last chink of sunlight in the

corner of the lawn after tea; the silver moonbeams of night when her ghost comes to find me. She's the sound of my parent's old wooden gate shutting in the lane; the

feel of soft warm flesh through silk in August rain. The taste of Charentais melons and crab apple pies cold from the fridge; sometimes I close my eyes and she's

the rails of a small wooden footbridge. At home she's a shrine of old clothes locked in a drawer; three rings on my antique phone in my purple corridor. She haunts the

lingering smoke of snuffed out strawberry candles fallen by my bed; she's a thousand words under my pillow, in my book, inside my head.

Rust; dust; the tissue paper petals of dried flowers; hours and hours and hours of longing, belonging in the voids of wasted love.

SUMMER 1995

Ah, to be bathed a last time in that love I knew as a child,
Only this time with the lame ghosts of those summers gone by;
And I can walk along their paths and angles,
Hide in the shade of their candy trees,
See my shadows lengthen across the garden,
In a play no- one left alive can see.

I still try to play tennis on the lawn, but the clovers are wild,
The numerals cracked and incomplete,
Paint peeling in the sun as the clock ticks past six forty five;
The gold of a July evening,
The breath of a life gone by.

Kites fly high on the horizon, searching for breeze,
Neighbours walk by, intrigued by my eccentric movements;
On the t.v, Agassi and Wheaton battle still more,
While out here I know I'm two match points down,
As time begs again to close the door.

And those down there who hold the power, they can have it;
They'll take this place away from me soon,
But these evenings will live forever in my head,
Long after the possessions in their loveless corridors
Have rusted and crumbled,
And those who bore me with their talk are all dead.

AUGUST 16th 1993

A bridge. Fields. Trees. A girl.
A silent movie, mine.
A tiny glass window, a spy- hole
Into a day that only I can live again.
But how many times can this eyepiece
Well up with tears?
I dare not watch her in colour:
To see through my eyes
The colour of her eyes
Would be too much;
Black and white keeps things separate,
Abstract.
I remember the previous evening,
When she lay next to me,
Naked, warm and sleepy,
Singing *This Is My Heart*,
Following the night
Into dream;
She, an apple picker
Rescuing me
From the high tree tops
Where I'd shouted
To the dead
Of the bliss I'd found;
The dream where I fell
And woke up in her arms:
The dream I never dreamt again.
Roses of three summers ago
Now lie dried and flaking
Above my bed
In remembrance;
A bridge. Fields. Trees. A girl.
A silent movie, mine.

RUNAWAY GIRL

So how come you became one of the disappeared?
A girl in the rain, walking a street somewhere;
The queen of oblivion.
I still have the pictures; I still wear the necklace you stole for me
When you couldn't afford a loaf of bread:
How sweet, and how bitter- sweet the memory.
Perhaps you became what you always wanted to be:
A heroine, lamented and immortalised
In monotone like a movie star;
Photographs of a smile and those so perfect, searching eyes;
Lips I've traced the outline of a thousand times
In the candle- lit gloom of my faded tie- dyes.
I've studied you more now you're gone
Than ever I dared to when you were by my side
In that bizarre relationship of sorts
I thought would never end.
Why did you let others drive you away?
I loved you.
I used to dream that you'd died, wake up in frozen panic.
I still do.
And there's all those songs you've missed:
Sullen Girl, Opium, Talula;
Is it true that you wrote me a hundred letters,
Never daring to send them?
Well, I wish you'd sent just one.
Were we both too mean to tell the truth?
Or too frightened?
And what of now?
Like the burnished moon through my window tonight,
You're so far away,
Yet your soft
Silver light still illuminates;
In here,
Filling the voids you left behind;
Perhaps this is what I always wanted:
Some twisted justification
For my hours of nothing,
Some lost girl,
Drowning in the blur
Of my undying confusion.
Tonight,
Rachel,
In this cold, rusted shrine;
You live.

BLACK ROSES

The high town walks are empty today,
And in the grey washes,
The church bells ring for no- one,
In this ghost town,
This emptiness.

People pass by below,
Unaware of the longing,
The loss;
This hillside of graves,
Lies frozen in tears,
And I'll soon be left behind,
Again.

Somewhere,
Far beyond my horizon,
Confetti rains.

NURSE

She lived inside my cupboard,
And in the last light of evening
She would stand beside me,
Taking obscure photographs;
Burning greenish as I came undone...
She'd cry,
Then she'd fly away,
Leaving tropical tears:
Lavender leaves
Crumbling under my pillow,
To be gathered
By doctors in daylight
Pronouncing me dead.

HAIKU TIME

Do I seem younger
By the light of your candle
Or can't you see me

LAST DREAM

You close the door. It's quiet. You turn to look at
me. You smile; I smile. You're still exactly as you
were: a girl lost in space, wearing my black shirt,

unbuttoned in suggestion. The ceiling is so low,
the window so small. It's warm, I wonder if your body
still tastes of cherries. In the light of a lone candle,

your eyes shine like slow motion pools of blue in
dying twilight. I speak. I say, *I love you.* You whisper,
I know. Strawberry light turns our bodies into day

and night, as I watch your breasts rise and fall; your
head tilt back; your arms reach out towards me like
the sun. I hold you; you clasp me tight. Mirrored,

here in deepest red, in a world perfumed with the
scent of August roses; we turn to liquid.

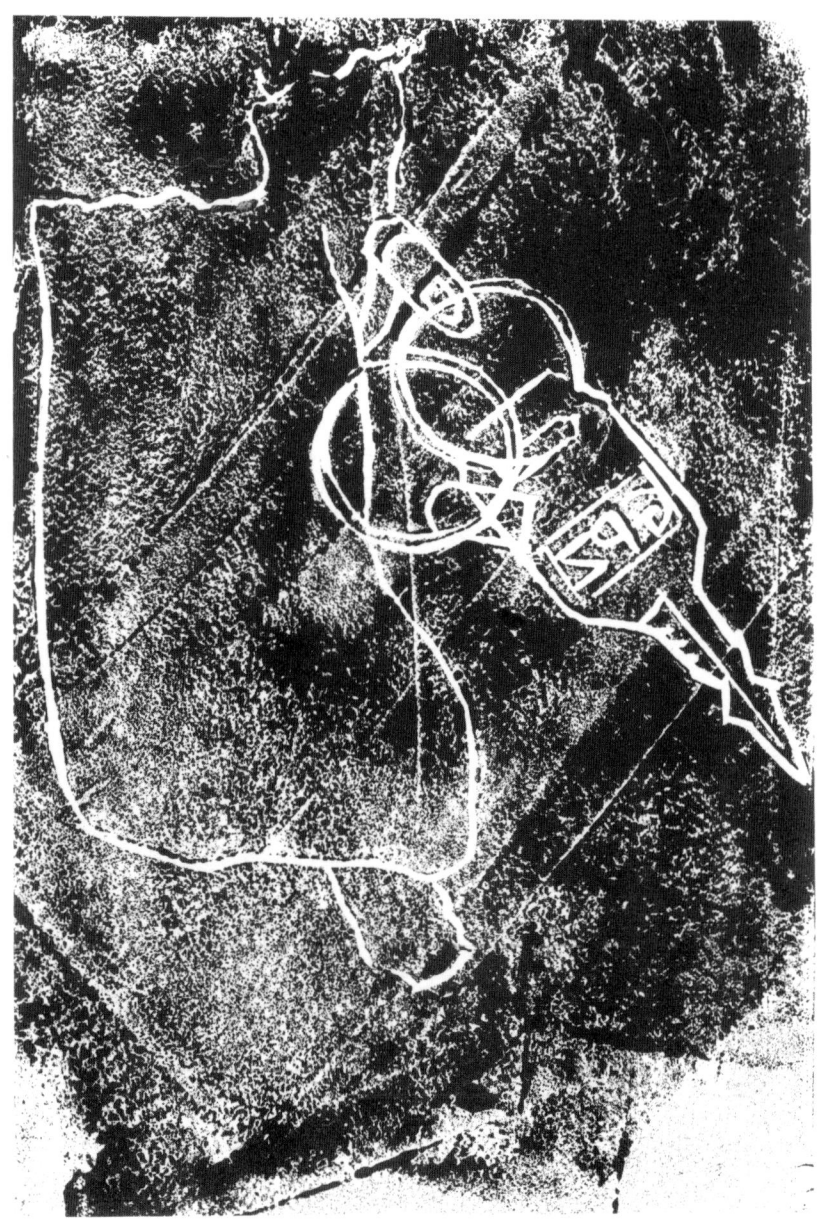

NURSE

She lived inside my cupboard,
And in the last light of evening
She would stand beside me,
Taking obscure photographs;
Burning greenish as I came undone...
She'd cry,
Then she'd fly away,
Leaving tropical tears:
Lavender leaves
Crumbling under my pillow,
To be gathered
By doctors in daylight
Pronouncing me dead.

HAIKU TIME

Do I seem younger
By the light of your candle
Or can't you see me

LAST DREAM

You close the door. It's quiet. You turn to look at
me. You smile; I smile. You're still exactly as you
were: a girl lost in space, wearing my black shirt,

unbuttoned in suggestion. The ceiling is so low,
the window so small. It's warm, I wonder if your body
still tastes of cherries. In the light of a lone candle,

your eyes shine like slow motion pools of blue in
dying twilight. I speak. I say, *I love you.* You whisper,
I know. Strawberry light turns our bodies into day

and night, as I watch your breasts rise and fall; your
head tilt back; your arms reach out towards me like
the sun. I hold you; you clasp me tight. Mirrored,

here in deepest red, in a world perfumed with the
scent of August roses; we turn to liquid.

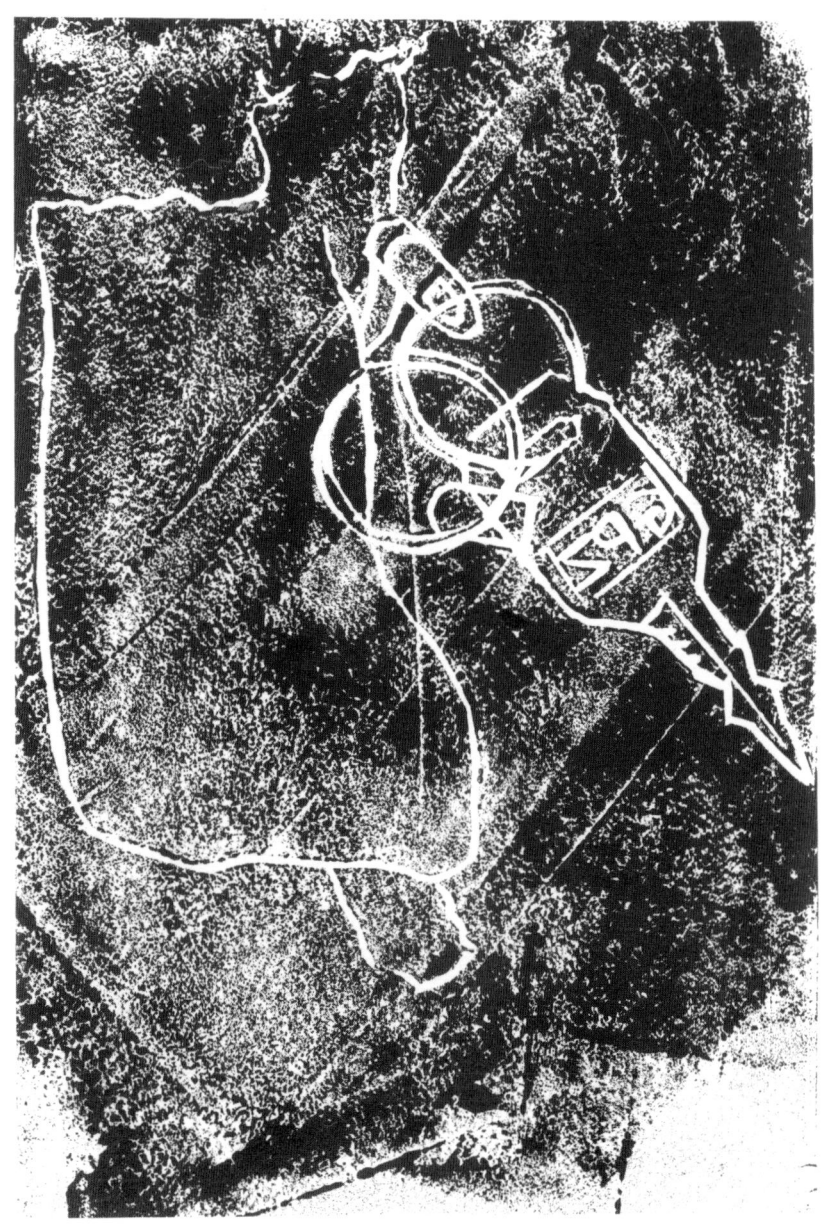

INFRARED HIGHWAYMAN

Do you remember
The sound of the last motorcycle
Echoing over the Lightwood fields
On a Friday night?
Did I wake you?
And did you curse me
As I fired past the Church Street Gardens
A mile away,
Before climbing Boundary bank
And fading into silence?
In dreams,
Is it still the sound
Of a lonely rider you long to hear?
Or can I go now,
Shut off the power,
Free wheel,
Disappear?

ACKNOWLEDGEMENTS

The author would like to thank:

Dave Edwards, for help and support. For being my friend and neighbour for twenty five years. Thanks also for letting me include a quote from the poem "Without You" in the front of this book.

Becky Martin, for her time and effort creating the images that accompany many of my poems. For her friendship over the last four years.

Hilary Jefferies, for her front cover image of my most treasured necklace and the "Infrared Highwayman" print. For her enthusiasm.

Rachel Stevenson, for being my "Runaway Girl", my most delicate muse and precious best friend. For her understanding of the great blue voids of my mind. For being the sole reason behind me creating this book, which is hers only, but most of all, for not disappearing again. I love you.

The author would also like to thank:

Katie Leigh, Kellianne Murray, Carla Hall, Gemma Hall, Nikki Kirkham, Roy Swanwick, Andrew Williams, Andrea Burton, Mike Simcock, Lee Poyser, Bob Wood, Leslie Hulse, Ross Lucas, Paul Beeston, Janet Thirlwall, Sarah Thirlwall, Ian Beeston, John Simpson, Lorraine, Lisa Greatorex, Rich Cope, Nick Cumberbatch, Andrew Morris, Eliot, Sophie Delawney, Henry, Honey, Lisa Kirkham, Maria Harvey.

And not forgetting:

The Brothers Ralphs: Andy "Mark Waugh" Ralphs and David "Skip Rat" Ralphs. Mum and dad and relatives in Longton, Worcester and Liverpool.

And staff at the following:

Williamson's Photographers in Longton, Stoke-on-Trent.
Rowfers Clothing in Hanley, Stoke-on-Trent.
Staffordshire University Bookshops.

This book was started in the gloom of January 1996 and was finished on a beautiful July evening in 1997, same day Steve Waugh scored 85 not out against England, Novotna lost the Wimbledon final, temperatures hit the mid seventies and the last photograph in this book was taken. This picture, along with extra poems and drawing by Rachel can be found in a "Hidden Away" section of post-scripts which follow this page.

INFRARED HIGHWAYMAN

Do you remember
The sound of the last motorcycle
Echoing over the Lightwood fields
On a Friday night?
Did I wake you?
And did you curse me
As I fired past the Church Street Gardens
A mile away,
Before climbing Boundary bank
And fading into silence?
In dreams,
Is it still the sound
Of a lonely rider you long to hear?
Or can I go now,
Shut off the power,
Free wheel,
Disappear?

ACKNOWLEDGEMENTS

The author would like to thank:

Dave Edwards, for help and support. For being my friend and neighbour for twenty five years. Thanks also for letting me include a quote from the poem "Without You" in the front of this book.

Becky Martin, for her time and effort creating the images that accompany many of my poems. For her friendship over the last four years.

Hilary Jefferies, for her front cover image of my most treasured necklace and the "Infrared Highwayman" print. For her enthusiasm.

Rachel Stevenson, for being my "Runaway Girl", my most delicate muse and precious best friend. For her understanding of the great blue voids of my mind. For being the sole reason behind me creating this book, which is hers only, but most of all, for not disappearing again. I love you.

The author would also like to thank:

Katie Leigh, Kellianne Murray, Carla Hall, Gemma Hall, Nikki Kirkham, Roy Swanwick, Andrew Williams, Andrea Burton, Mike Simcock, Lee Poyser, Bob Wood, Leslie Hulse, Ross Lucas, Paul Beeston, Janet Thirlwall, Sarah Thirlwall, Ian Beeston, John Simpson, Lorraine, Lisa Greatorex, Rich Cope, Nick Cumberbatch, Andrew Morris, Eliot, Sophie Delawney, Henry, Honey, Lisa Kirkham, Maria Harvey.

And not forgetting:

The Brothers Ralphs: Andy "Mark Waugh" Ralphs and David "Skip Rat" Ralphs. Mum and dad and relatives in Longton, Worcester and Liverpool.

And staff at the following:

Williamson's Photographers in Longton, Stoke-on-Trent.
Rowfers Clothing in Hanley, Stoke-on-Trent.
Staffordshire University Bookshops.

This book was started in the gloom of January 1996 and was finished on a beautiful July evening in 1997, same day Steve Waugh scored 85 not out against England, Novotna lost the Wimbledon final, temperatures hit the mid seventies and the last photograph in this book was taken. This picture, along with extra poems and drawing by Rachel can be found in a "Hidden Away" section of post-scripts which follow this page.

ON TIMBERDELL
APRIL 16th 1997

So time has taken me to this hillside, this view; what do I see?
Endless fields, sweep of hills, roads leading out like streams to
places we never needed or saw, and which I now view as soft

discoloration on a far horizon. The gold they use to colour in
old movies is here in plenty, but I cannot save it, it's too late. Too
late for me - a time traveller who's returned to this beloved place

to find only disintegration. I can still see your old house from here,
your father's car parked in the drive in the late evening sun; from
here everything's unchanged, that's why I don't want to walk away...

Among the foxgloves and jasmine, high on Timberdell, out here on
the Leek Road in a place where no- one could find me, I've run
aground. Too late to do any other than watch the street lights reveal

the hamlets and tributaries that lie before me, like solutions to puzzles
in the back of a book... *this book*, where at least one day I know I'll
find you looking. Perhaps then, in some strange fashion, you'll be able

to share with me this moment; this future day; this late night picture show;

And these words are all I can ever leave here for you,
it's too late, too late I know.

SUMMER SNOW (SONG)

Five O' clock in the morning
Through my kitchen window snow fallin'
Buttoned up my jacket
Felt the cold air of winter again
Walking over Calverhay
In fields of snow white as cocaine

Crossed the river by the train tracks
Leaving Abram's Bridge far behind
Through the mist and coloured ice
I threw away all my dreams
Left them for someone else to find

Take me away, baby
Away from this black snow filled sky
I can't walk on frozen streams
Can't wake from broken dreams
Anymore
You know I tried every spell
In every book I could find
To survive
But they only made me miss you more

Saw the rainbow turn the sky blood red
Saw it land in fields of beet root
And borage turned grey like lead
I remembered your voice callin' me
On the telephone in the dead of night
Turned and saw only my own footsteps
Darlin', leadin' way out of sight

For years I've seen others go
Over the fields where the wolf vines grow
I watched them win and lose their race
Left me cold and out of place
As these fields of summer snow

Take me away, baby
Away from this black snow filled sky
I can't melt these frozen streams
Can't wait on broken dreams
Anymore

Rachel A.K.A. "8" July '97
Photo by Ian A.K.A. "△"
further reading: Kristin Hersh "Me & my charms",
Mazzy Star "Roseblood" & MSG "Nightmare"